LILAC CIGARETTE IN
A WISH CATHEDRAL

*Publication of this book was supported by a grant from
the Eric Mathieu King Fund of The Academy of American Poets.*

THE
James
DICKEY
CONTEMPORARY POETRY SERIES

EDITED BY RICHARD HOWARD

LILAC CIGARETTE IN
A WISH CATHEDRAL

Poems by Robin Magowan

UNIVERSITY OF SOUTH CAROLINA PRESS

© 1998 Robin Magowan

Published in Columbia, South Carolina, by the
University of South Carolina Press

Manufactured in the United States of America

02 01 00 99 98   5 4 3 2 1

Library of Congress Cataloging-in-Publication Data

Magowan, Robin.
  Lilac cigarette in a wish cathedral : poems / by Robin Magowan.
    p. cm. — (The James Dickey contemporary poetry series)
    ISBN 1-57003-269-6. — ISBN 1-57003-270-X (pbk.)
    I. Title. II. Series.
  PR6063.A329L55 1998
  821'.914—dc21   97-45433

in memory of James Merrill

CONTENTS

A NOTE ON ROBIN MAGOWAN

One of the most difficult tasks which literary art has assumed or perhaps in modernity been *assigned* is the recuperation of ecstasy. The notation of what has been grasped—given, granted: a grace that cannot be asked or bidden—by the senses only to transcend them is particular function or contemporary literature, sustaining intimate relations with the religious and the erotic, even with the blasphemous and the pornographic, as the instances of Henri Michaux and William Burroughs confirm.

Prose is the expedient medium, of course, but a problematic one as well. Boundaries must be continuously sealed off, yet this is in prose a hopeless task, for everything touches everything else; a beginning never disappears, not even with an ending. Poetry, then—that ceremony of edges which we have come to call *verse,* in especial—will be the engine best actuating such an impulse, a way of cropping, framing, setting apart a seized state: often, on Magowan's occasions, a seizure indeed, drug-propelled and drastic in its descending consequences. Yet he has other occasions, essays of immediate contemplation, what Virginia Woolf (and Thomas Hardy) called Moments of Vision, and it is worth noting how diligently this poet prepares himself, actually reconnoiters his means in order to be ready for their onset. There is a long foreground of focusing, condensing, clarifying (as the chefs say), before we get to the consecrated period:

> . . . No one talks.
> Sweeping hands, wind-red faces,
> A boy blowing flute-like into a grate
> Where tea and potatoes steam.
>
> I step out to a blackness
> So transparent the quarter moon

Illumines the line of my path
Mounting past farms and bare fields.
Everything seems to be waiting.
I feel very thin, alone, joyful.

Then it happens to him, the illumination arrives, and it is the poet's duty to get out of the way of these privileged moments, to restrict any sort of *personal claim;* a certain wild patience will be the characteristic attitude and the winning stance, vigilant but not possessive, and then the ecstatic (*standing outside the self,* after all) can occur:

    . . . I wanted
    And my wishes were creams, stranded.
    I wanted and my tongue emerged
    From its bath, a raven croaking.
    I wanted and what I couldn't suppress
    I became . . .

The poet Claudel has made a great to-do over the relation of knowing (*connaissance*) and to being born (*naissance*). I should like to avoid the doctrinal subtleties of his overpowering arguments, but hold on to the insight bestowed, for Magowan's performance of the immediate (there have been many rehearsals: journeys taken and recorded, translations made, studies of genre laboriously pursued, submissions of all kinds) is indeed a kind of birth, a way of being born to Now. And now is knowledge in this poetry, the only learning to be valued, for it affords the consequences, the *rewards* of all this transparency, the often dangerous apprenticeship to self-suppression, indenture to an apparently religious (yes, but not ecclesiastical) humility:

    Risen through the orchard
    A moon husk to light my way.
    I liberate myself from silences.
    As I step I am.

I must acknowledge that with the powers he assumes come the eccentricities of power, the oddities of being all that open. How else account for a title as peculiar as Magowan's? But that's just it, there may be no question of accounting, only the answers of accepting; "the hours wait, unseen, heavy" and the hierophant smokes his lilac cigarette in a wish cathedral. Of course he does. What else could he do, making those "fragrant pauses / of white / discovery"?

Richard Howard

SAILOR AT PEREMA

Fingers snapping,
Priest in a dream of stones,
He sketches out his dance.
Maybe someone very blank, tall,
Cucumber-shouldered,
Will stand alongside, hold out
His handkerchief. Around him
The dream turns / turns
Like milk, dispersing
Out of thin white trousers
Quietude
Elation
Manna.
The two move, circling, as on the rim
Of a glass: hands, fat
Soft-spinning flowers; feet
Spokes in a cycle of prayers.
They speak in a tongue of rain
Sensing the hands all around
Breaking in green time like plates.

PAROS

The road spins, high on a waist, its way
Threaded through transparencies of sea-
Whitened olives. Fields ripple out, tiers
Of green and gold speckled with poppies—
As many poppies as green stalks of wheat—
Maybe in a corner the lone cube
Of a farmhouse binding fields and sea
In a white flowing salve.
                      The roadway
Glimmers like a sword, the eye sheering
Downwards past little blue-domed houses,
Terraced, with steps like lumps of sugar,
To where in a pot of flame the sea
Funnels the light's last oils, the houses
Reaching their whites down to it like tongues
And up over the cobbles the lime
Drawing it, skywards, like a first breath,
Promise of infinite accession
And happiness.
                  Soft smoke is in the voice
Singing with the sea in the pebbles
Of his mouth, the sound high, honeylike,
Reaching over the bay with that flat
Even insistency of serpents
Over grass, until some fisherman
Gets up from his table—hissing—his arm
A mast moving in a white vortex
Over the floor, eyes down, the slow circles
Descending, searching, the sea with him
Naming her, the sound a thread downwards
Through the spool of hisses guiding him as
He steers over its tilting sun-dialed frame
And light pours in swords into him, melting
The streets into a wax, while the head, dis-
Membered, floats out over the singing stones.

2

CYTHERA

The island
Turns in its fired indigo and sings
The air is swimming
Shadows that scurry
Or lie in knifebright trance
And I want not one stone
Removed not one lizard

A black frantic absorption of shallows
Cards like caïques
Slapping against table
And the forks speak
And the donkey rags go home
And only I am left
Cup myself in my mouth of sunlight

Asking only that tomorrow may find me
Smooth as paper round as stone
Days will redden on my chest
Lips like a spade will darken
And the autumn an old mill
We forks and donkey rags
Carrying what our soles have trod stamped
While a double-stringed music with drum
And under the wrists white tiny bells
Weaves dissolves on the quickneedle wind
Pointed shoes red moonlight
I any night dancing

PORTRAIT OF THE
PAINTER KALDIS

Your olympus
rises out of paper
purple in the flush of rain
with a golden cap
& brows of curling juniper. Each
touch brings an explosion
of cypress & thumb-pressed
olive trees
against which the red,
blue houses stand atilt
in a splatter of white-
hued steps.
In the silence the breath
of a courtyard broom swings,
swings & becomes sailcloth, bay
full of kelp, bathing suits,
oven-green laughter.
And the mountain writhes
afloat in a dream of lava,
slopes gathering meadows
poppy-singed
where only the breadth
of a cypress sways
& invisible
among almonds
a ploughman whistles.

TAPESTRY

A stork sits in his spoon of shadow
As the olive trees salaam
Their beaded blues,
Grays, dolphin over
A tinder of bright
Basket yellows, stitched
Thick with horses, goats,
Figs, rooster-
Colored houses,
Under an oak the bell
Of a shepherd boy, silver shirted, asleep.
The hours wait, unseen, heavy.
In blue, a harbor,
Oyster in the still
Pointed sun.

Woven in
The stork wakes
To wavering brook-
Cobbled lanes
Courtyard whose loukoum whites
Open onto red
Blossoming pomegranates,
A gateway's hand reaching out
Cupped, promising.
He takes it, head
Bent, wing sleeves
Bowing.
He is dancing, drawing

Her under his huge soft beak,
Her eyelids
Archways where bees crawl
And scents thicken.

NOON TAVERNA

Secrecies
of air—
wine
and flies.

PAVAN IN A MYOPIC KEY

Hope at the end of evening
When the tree's vessels have collapsed
And dawn breaks, throat a horse touches,
Heals. Your long-boned finger hangs down
And jangles, musical as glass,
As the cups of shadowed hillside
Above which your mountains rise,
A skating line of sudden ash-
Pointed leaps over a sea
Clean as silk.
Around you water swells,
A purse out of which a million insects should float
And the sun, rising, disclose not breasts
But the palest of blue eggs
On whose lids mosquitos press
Very softly
As if laying sun-cakes.
Your heart is a pomegranate
Whose each blossom bursting
Becomes a blur spread like some raincoat
In whose folds microscopic ships glow
And a dowitcher pointedly gurgles.

TSAMIKO

The journey's chain winds, unwinds, our hands
Drunken plates in a sea of viscous blues,
Reds, perspiration, prayers,
Suddenly we stop, stamp three times,
Entering where the river mouth opens
Heavy, thick with eels,
And a village thrusts flagpole beaks in tall
Saw-colored air. Here
Hopes come to feed
And the days glitter
Days in which the dream, sylvan, hangs
Spattering warm juices upon anvil soil.
Thrush call in the tide loops
And over Mycenae a music shrills
The men moving storklike
Arms hoops
Disks of silver as one
Another drops, touches hand & spins
Leaping, the clarino's notes
Grapes wherein we stand
Humble, close to extinction,
Blue sunguided sound.

ZEMBEIKIKO

An old peasant gets up turns
As in his own hen-scuttled yard
He is breaking it
Yard fields family stoneroofed house
Takes steps on makes with his hands
Fuse of a cigarette crackle sing
In the ash of his glass dancing
The floor a round white over which he stoops
Hops twice JUMPS!
Sizzle of browns
Blacks
Flash of a horsewhip
Stubble-bright falling

Zembeikiko
Says it His is
Hisses He takes something round
Shape of a palm and with it hits
Smashes: floor trousers shoes white-of-nail
Dark he scoops slices spins
Is manna is hands sunwhip and stone
Is the man who says No I'm not
Old Coocoocoorooooo
Who suncaps shoes
And washes the stones in the verminous oxides of night
And stands tongue of crow floorblack hands shouting
I HANDS RAIN COME
LOOKING FOR YOU DADDY
WHO GAVE ME THIS NAME WORM
A giant fist dances sings
And a tray of ouzo glasses descends
Shoes plates hair glittering phosphorescent shirts
Through which he mosquito bright glides
White   dipping

Moving over all the floor

                           moving
                           threshing
                           sowing

I am me he says *I burn the knife I cry*
Wings soar and melt
The fire
Is the globe I am

DESPAIR

Despair, great tree,
With your hands turned outwards like sockets
Your shoulders of moss and wet shining cones
Saying, *My direction is set, downwards.*
I shall bury the earth with my prongs.
Despair, long-toothed comb, which coats and subdues
Without multiplication tables
Only the senses breathing
Cobra-headed
Grebes floating on their own disks
Beaks outstretched
Probing the glisten where the moon is salt
And islands plunge past
Shot with silk and the mahoganies of silence;
Tall once, but so long borne in the cycles
Only their fir crests remain
And these too threatening to dissolve
White writing
Moss of a forest matting
That's also a huge tenement
Trees growing out of other trees and others waiting
Skinny uptilted would-be basketball players;
So numerous I end by replacing them with woodpeckers.
In their beaks' fire I turn
My wings shining with the iridescence of salmon
As they move over a glass
They fill with their tiny needles
Of dazzling fist-scented rain.

BIRTH

for Felix

Knots of light speckle the hospital wall
while I gaze at the headlights
aglow in the fishmouth dark
as day like a grove of oranges
begins to dawn. Attendants
drift in, but nothing can be done,
nothing that won't stop your coming.
Sixteen hours later you come
bearing the wand
and as you strike
the screams
sing
and dusk
is cut in sandwiches
of green and gold. Threads
wind out of our eyes
where you lie stretched
across her belly's amber
as in a vial of oil:
mouth wide and twisted like a harp
eyes color of
distant firs and mountains
corners tilting like small pontoons.
Later, behind nursery glass
blue mitten hands stir
in their tidepool sleep, starfish
searching, and with blind eyes
you wade
seeking your length of gum-
green water like the answer
to some dream of distant raft and
sunlight
thistle and thigh-white cloud.

IN SUSAN'S ROOM

A moment before class and I scribble this
Into the nineteen year horizon
      Of your eyes
Your long moon-dreaming hands, your breath
Which, when it isn't salt, wants roses
      To come and
      Settle
On the blank sheath of your skin
      Where each pore
Opens & closes itself & becomes fence
      Skirt, meadow
    And the colors of all Susan
      All fish, all
      Bright ladders
In the sum of your white & laughing face

MINIATURE

The pleasure of sounds innocently grasped
A peacock in the eyes of the rain

WIND

Wind curls around cliffs riding out tide
Wind curls in hawk eyries—you'll go away I'll never see you
Wind curls under pines bringing wine lice hair
Sucking it up to my eyes
Bringing a moose rain oh how I love him
Wind dashes slashes the rock levels
Slops hair wet green washes it down flip-flop
Seal cry toss of wave oh how I love him
Wind curls in back of sea bone
Pulling me like rock like wave like translucent new skin
Wind curls in back of foam among leaf boulders
Crash your fist where I stoop
Wanting you to flavor me with your hand
Wanting the long arrow the red cunning cleaning wound
Wanting you to deliver me from eye
Sound of eye on the wave glass
To clean my armpits of algae
To meadow my hair with red luck
To feast in my bed of bone and break it
Hands over wrists mouth under my love car
Oh how I love you beast flapping wings over my embers
And I lighting up meadow waves proudly
Orange spume come come
Breaking over me like rainbow salt
Silvering my arms' mist
Granting me being open as rain
Blush in my bush of clouds

CONSOLATIONS OF BOURBON

Appalled at our four-year charade
"Too few" "not at all"
In the garden dusk counting them
The hours before I must leave our house
Your eyes' sword points
Locked in that jail's "too few," "not at all."
I want to leave you doors
That close when they do not open
The house I erected for my bird friend
The pasture where you dropped the lazy silk of your behind
And I fondled it "too few," "not at all."
I went to stopper this sink to your despair
To hold my hand bright-fisted again
To sheathe every wind and bone
In the crying banks where I yaw
Helm in the green sand grinding.
Suddenly I hear, you don't want, you are
Stick of your own passion wanting night
A hen to clobber, a cloud to burst
Dark, cylindrical, in that dripping wilderness
Where I take you to my breast
And the stars murmur and the rain descends.

BEFORE A SECOND HYSTERECTOMY

—for Dodi Kho

Dream the Cycladic dawn, the windmills, the shadow knives,
A noon that erases everything but the crying of number one,
"Some pleasure before I croak,"
And you unable to extend the railing of a hand.
"Life is too short," you say
And the stars come out and you sit admiring them
Not dreaming they may be reflections of your eyes
Coca-Cola hard in airport dust
Intent only on Düsseldorf, a rain two days away.
You are dumb, brutalized by history, and brutalized by
    yourself,
That way of wiping all light from your eyes
And substituting a cigarette
Your avenue to the stars. So smoke,
Kindle yourself into the likeness of thought,
Of music, the cigarette
Flute and we all believing the pipe sounds
That mean nothing but evil
A life that, not given, seldom returns.

LOOKING FOR BINOCULARS

At the back of a Point Reyes ravine
Mescaline, three powdery silver piles
Poured on knife blades and then and there licked clean.
Remorse rising geometrically
Directs us ever more briskly around
Two bends and in the nick onto a bush-
Lupin meadow. Taking Ling by the arm
I guide her up to the bluff's fire-mist view.
Nausea. Urge to jettison sweaters,
Binoculars' black encumbering holes.
"I want to bail out, get away!" I shriek.
But much as I'd like to, there is nowhere
To bail out past an imprisoning sky
The chalk-circle clouds tearing us
Leather apes in the jungle of our fears.

Edge to meadow ledge I roll, mouth, dagger,
Precipice, star, as each diving phaeton
Unloads its dizzy, screaming, sun-abyss.
Electrons the size of golfballs diffract
As I wriggle to where my Circe sprawls
Elbows over eyes, black paint-spattered jeans
Rotating at washing machine frenzy.
Through the churn I hear her voice her chagrin,
"Sorry, I've poisoned you, more TNT
Than I've ever imagined." But her voice
Clatter proves too much and I roll away
Preferring my own wretched wastes and heaves.

To find a middle and cling: letter "M"
Well beloved of the French; Ling's navel,
Cavity into which I can intrude
All I possess of mouth, of roots. Cocooned
In exploding infancy—stars direct

To tonguelost Babel?—I lie, arms twined,
Letting only my most fervent Allahhh's
Shower forth their groaning sparks. I'm reaching back
Mothering island where, what heart once knew,
Tongue gives out: <u>beast, breast</u>; meadowed ring, found.

We cling, each's wheel and axle, until
The same instant's grasslight finds us sitting
Rubbing eyes before its huge, blue-streaked blades.
Beneficence shines. Do I catch the song
The brothers sang approaching the well? Yet
Everything is, it all startles so;
The moist flower beads, the brook in the wild.
Do you pull me into sunlight, your touch
Making wax grow solid? Behind lupin
I stand relieving myself, head in hands,
Invisible legs vibrating like stalks.

"Time," Ling announces, "to leave that blue place."
My shoes stand up, their laces tied and all.
Jeans are sparkling blue on pink gravel road.
Arms seem to limp at sides, but this may be
Because I can't focus on my fingers
Lost in the mist prism; nor the roadway
Though like a sleepwalker I recognize
A blue balustrade curving to my right.
Useless to ponder what is dream, what walk;
After wriggling in wet ghostly grass
Being erect is miracle enough.

"Where are your binoculars?" Ling's question
So out of the blue has me frantically
Combing the bluff as if I've mislaid them.
I'm set to drop into the poison oak
Below (they could have rolled over the ledge)
When she adds, "Your other pair is lost too."
Back we walk, a hole with a head, two heads,

Looking for a hole between there and here.
And a title, as much an afternoon's
As a hotel sign, comes into focus.
Looking for binoculars: falling off
Of hole. Finding them: standing by a well?

At the meadow edge a conflagration
Of sunset-lit poppies drops us to knees.
I have Ling's hand, this future fire power,
Might binoculars prove superfluous?
On elbows, kids at a concert, we sprawl.
While Ling paints I scan her fingertip,
Pink hemisphere of desires, as if
A stroke might reveal the gold of my face
Beckoning from lily pad to the swamp's
Cleopatra. But the comparison
Palls among the waning light's still unfound
Binoculars. Bluff's glistening of wind,
Crashing of assassin waves, as we comb
The holes of our earlier foot pressings.
Through spray, her dejected 'I can't find them'
As crashings foam around. Alone again.
A roaring, a black cataract of stars.
An afternoon, two bodies pulling one
Another through, lies on its back, blown up.

"Hurry!" stars are all quavering as one.
But deep in a windproof ravine I pause
Transfixed by a pool the moonrise's ping-
Pong is furling to an undersea grotto.
Below, minuscule brass buttons startle.
Across, soil leathers, alderbark grays merge.
Swaying together, they rise in a mushroom
Blowing, separate, subside. Stuffs glisten:
Tree bark silks; satiny water a cow-
Parsley's cathedral stalks reflect
And eyes, on a reel, spool from blank to bank.

I'm not disconnected from anything
Not even my sea anemone arms
That, writhing with each pulse, call it night,
A deeper purple I can't pierce beyond.

Shadows like a liner's bow dock my veins.
But so long as pupils glow with this firelight
I must remain out. In the gloom, branch low,
Wobble flutter of a first whippoorwill!
Through glittering reeds my feet thrash drowning
Before bursting onto a knoll over-
Looking the swell's radiator-long coils,
Jagged kelp sticks agleam like purple glass.
Then the surf starts to heave away from me
The station lights spit and, needing shelter,
I sprawl among the roots of a monster
Cypress. Snug I lie, letting my eye straws
Gulp the radiances, pink, red, blue-white;
Not constellations, but glistening webs
As if each sky shepherd holds alignments
It tenders to those harbored in its mist.
Webs drip until arrayed enough I stand
Stalk my way back through the sabering night.

MOSAIC FROM THE FLOOR OF THE DESIGN

From the night of Chief Tomahawk
        Ravaged brain cells
Wake to a lagoon innocent
        As glass. Circling,
On our way to those gaping holes
        Binoculars
Jettisoned on the bluff meadow
        We halt for signs
The startled, soft-fused signalings
        Of the poppy
And buttercup peoples bivouacked
        Against grass, fence
Posts, sky. Does the kingfisher on
        Firepole keep
The mirror from gaping open?
        A great heron
Glides down, fish blue as the morning
        Held out in claws.
Far, on a sandspit, flapping white
        Accordion
Wings, dancing egrets starflames to
        Sway with, pull in.
On foot we reach a vernal pool's
        Salamander
Congress, a hundred randy fire
        Bellies fucking.
As Ling stoops under a willow
        To peer, her mane,
A blue-black waterfall, plummets
        An explosion
Of incendiary light-and-
        Grass-filled chartreuse.

DEATH VALLEY

Campground. Winter wind.
You, cauliflower of surfaces
I have some trouble to bind.
Why do I need hope so?
Wouldn't a clear eye do
My door open to a knock from anywhere?
If I owned my kindness and sowed
All along the wind's rivers
The forces braided in dark
Now embering out: porcupine, wood smoke
Gathered from the breaches
Ice I cook, turn into needles, sew,
Eye, lone maker of an original world.
So long, were it not for stars,
I couldn't see love's pattern on the chesscloth,
Ropes tender as skin I take down
Fold where your picture smokes, grinning.
I see our days together gathered up, up,
"Heaven help me!" screamed at you I adore
Commonplace moon of my life.
I drag bedding into your glow
Place my heart down.
Lie, o.k., what next?
A cloudburst, I crawl back under
Hoping the bumpity-bump-bump of the train
To sleep is no more than the tent's chattering
Praying for a kinder hour.
As I'm murmuring this trash
From up the slope I hear a witchy cackle.
Is it my death laughing in the way train wheels
Sometimes laugh creaking through the long desert?
Will I stumble my way there
Measuring the sun by the rays it expressly
Lets fall? What if my lips too were a sun

Licking the gold flowering there like lamb
Washing their shadows in salt and their moon in convulsions
Heart for whom there are only moments
Movements of you and I gathered to an alien dream salt
Necks bowed and like sorrels drinking.
I'm the head I fold these ropes over
You the bitterness I must expunge
Because who, stooped to his ashes, wants another sun
Wringing me to my own tent, own rope, own skin.

INTRUDER IN
THE ABYSS

Mescaline evening.
Under red tongue
Lace willow this gem
Walk-sparkling.
Out over the water
Whirling silver dish castles
Irradiate a lake
Whose least wish is ice.
But the labials also frame
My lorelei's black hairstream bangs
Frogloud through temple garden
Flashing. Like a yo-yo her eyewhites
Draw me down, dins of foaming
Pounding iceshore lather,
Then up, saturn rings of silver night
Whose star yellows turn
Refract qualify one another
As Ling and I dancing might
Astride this lake-
Projecting bough
Enclenched cobras of night
"And of ourselves!" I exult
Grasping where, life in light,
We dive into carnivory becoming.
But as *d r o w n* bubbles up
The water breast separates
Temples of our twin-parted,
Twin-brushed, spreading
And engulfed shadows.

As I surface grasping
Rays translate me to a frost-
Emerald forest
Glade all encircling
Cobra-bough eyes hoods tongues
Controlled by spidery denizens
Out of themselves spinning a fiber
Moonlight of the hands I weave
Garden my way back to my lorelei.
But that stripper singer
Dodalesquing her tentacle pulpy breasts
(And their leaking cyclamates)
Has me whirring back out, sky's
Satined moonshudderings.
At zodiac's
Spinal Nerve Reverberator Zone
Gravity's yo-yo regrips.
Plummeting, lake eye looms
And I'm through, slope
Infernoing abyssward, only a last
Blossoming cherry branch
Snaps and it's me
          p e t a l i n g ?
Pedaling a movie's decibel hall
Whose marquee reads
          INTRUDER IN THE ABYSS
          BEAST WITH THE CHOCOLATE FROWN

HOPSCOTCH

I

oh joy, jumping up with lead
oh joy, mounting all my veins
to cobra a forest, cigarette ash my brains
oh joy, oh joy, neon crimson cigarettes
oh joy, oh joy, left hooks infinite
oh joy, oh joy, what prongs have you me on
oh joy, oh joy, jumping matchstick cigars
oh joy, oh joy, jumping funeral parlors
oh joy, oh joy, anything you can imagine
oh joy, oh joy, I-I-I cannot
oh joy, oh joy, go any longer
oh joy, oh joy, come to the end of my rope
oh joy, oh joy, jumping out of the moon
oh joy, oh joy, jumping, jumping
oh joy, oh joy, jumping funeral parlors
jumping, jumping, all along my mind
jumping, jumping, jumping funeral parlors

II

froggy bushes jump over your spine
froggy bushes in the Apennines
froggy bushes got a crater in his eye
jump all over his bushes jump all over his spine
froggy bushes all over your spine
froggy froggy froggy keeps them down
bushes bushes all over your spine
froggy froggy k-e-e-p-s them down
all over your bushes Apennines
froggy froggy keeping them that way
all over your bushes all over your spine

ONE-WAY-OUT TICKET

The junkstore. She waits outside
Her bandaid box of a home.
He steps in. She pours a sandwich,
Two nail slivers in one fried cream.
She has ghosts. She wants him to wait
Because the ghosts aren't out yet.
She's afraid he will go away.
People are such mice around her.
No, not eat them, just wash them
In her jelly until good and round
And hope someone arrives to light
Up her door of incense and smiles.
Bleak remedies sprout from her bed
Coal, plastic flowers, some coolaid.
She is Miss Hope in her Rothko dress
She tells herself, but even this
Game of clowns wears thin. Who now
Is she talking to through the mirrors?
Her lost life when she was an orange
Ball in Utah in the flaming dusk
Stepping out of her car, seeing him,
Saying "Hi!" in her flip-willow voice
Then retiring to await whatever
Might rebound in that extremity.
God? A silver john? Motel
Where the two crazily in love
Stayed a whole week? The witnesses
Were soft-spoken then, brought picnics
In rose baskets, looked under knees
And skirt for the flower tucked there
Never the same, precious few lately
She thinks reminded of the whipcord
She used climbing in Nevada
Plugging in where feet wouldn't grip

And hanging serenely for hours.
Later her home was Black Jock Rock.
Life seemed more open, less full
Of clothespins, she could have her way
Without having to pay in paisley
Sheets and doubled curlers: be
The brick you so desired.
I did. We shacked up down the hill
From Black Rock. Nights were cold there
Hips flared behind a pastry
She'd be fingering as she whispered
Excitedly to come, try
Some. We got fat together.
Lawns became lines we didn't mow.
Sleep-drenched mornings when the duck
Came out of her face and quacked
Evenings when we sat by a larch
And the honey poured over our hands
And our voices came out like stars
And we shone back and forth, husks
Of our dusk-extended quiet
As she saw-pressed her hips up
And I burst in, an illicit,
Secret addiction like a sun
In a fern forest as I dropped
My head and close-shouldered drank.
I drank your days of clear silver,
Your tongue thumping like rain, a kettle
About my lit, laughing sides.
My folly ebbed in light spurs
Picking a stalk and flowering it,
Wheat-thin arms, mad sugarbush
I entered, or lingered breathing
Outside, last pool before the break
Ensured disaster: plummeting
Waterfall of the green-gold eyes
Holding self to a nether world

While an open one umbrella'd
Memories of silks, starving
Fingers, stormworn hands. I wanted
And my wishes were creams, stranded.
I wanted and my tongue emerged
From its bath, a raven croaking.
I wanted and what I couldn't suppress
I became, these months passed in
A richness of uncommon thread.
But deny that, flash a signal,
"I hate to leave, I have to,"
And dissolve into that doorway
Where you stood, three rings on your hand
Sending cigarette flares
Into the tendril night, "Come
Into my being, spit upon me
Like rain," being a flower's
Indelicate ecstasy
While I stood slightly aside
And looked. Oh I was ashamed
That my hands felt so oily
Lighting up with a lagoon's
Crescent-headed loon, lighting
More out of fright than because
I was myself that cigarette
When left alone I crawled out
And the night glimmeringly
Shone. Its tender wakes I heard
Closing the cup and calling it
Sunday, closing to offer me
A one-way-out ticket, peck-peck
In my heart's leaves, touching them,
Then pointing to the cabin walls,
"I can't come with you, even if
I wanted to, and I don't."
Mice come and years devour the mice
And grief stays forever the same.

If I could bend a tire around
It, I would. Dogs would like it
And cigars from the old store days
Red heads to the light murmuring
Something about silence, the willow
That grows in the heat of the snow.
I too am a creature. I live
In the locked shadow of my heart.

PAGODA

As under a vast squatting woman
The pilgrim lies, hands pointed,
Touching, drumming.
Birds fly in, monkeys scamper,
From beam supports a girdle of carved
Gilt leaves and dog bodies thrusts
Inviting. Seven flights up
Roof is agleam, nodules
Quivering with each nod
Of a head. Bell twanged,
Prayer cask
Rotated, what matter! Or all
Matters in this rushing, river-
White breathing, "At the entrance
You, Vishnu, shall instill the whirl
As you do your temple pool,"
(Recumbent, whale-
Black on ocean leaf;
Supporting the dreamer's head
A raft of cobras
Tongues uplifted, wanting more
Fire, more sky: to be roasted,
Sucked, delivered
Into night, lavenders
Slipped into as into that kingdom
All sunken shadow and column-
Lined beneath the waves.
Darker, my temples glow, a ringing
Song forest guiding me to her bed
To be clad in those roses
Her lips will usher forth
Dawn-broken, smiling.

MORAINE

As I advance my glider-like bulk
Feet seem chasms away
Mouth a star

Gravitational pull
To teeter over, never sure when a rock
Will blast up like a woodcock.

As day warms
Streams loosen ice bonds
Fan out in marble toy transparencies;

Or a pond glitters
Drops of gold
In a vault sliced white by wind.

On overhangs, twice, porters
Separate from their load.
While we stand

Afraid even to talk
Our standard of living
Is solemnly retrieved.

The path owns only boulders
Jaws' crashing
Glittering

Where each mica shale
Strikes a paranoic note.
Why not stop

Sit and relax
How else remember?
By thinking

The train in the night
Train-path
I prod my sun along

In the fastness
Of the rising shadows.
Where everything is toted

Up-down must be a song
Hat on head, teeth
Aglitter in the chastening wind.

TESI LAPCHA PASS

Bright knocks to blue kingdom
Make mountains
A massive powdery rumbling
A turquoise shimmer's dripping arrows;
Pretexts to halt,
Extend breath to an unlit
Earth held in sky
Whose walker is but mist
Tomb in a valley, hope
Under a cloud.

Valley end's red and tan boulder wall.
Coughing, heads thrusting, shoulders pulling,
We mount, glove, knee, rock, eye,
Translucency to take an axe to,
Carve me, blue parka
Fitted to bright stone slab.

How in heelless boots
Our porters find cliffholds
I don't know, but hold they do
Trampling the snow a black-red-and-green.
Tongues protrude
And heads shake a lot as they walk.
The rest is heels,
Heels, a walking
Densely pronged with earth,
Necks bowed, goggled eyes turned down,
Crate borne like the very calf on the back.
Moving, shadow envelopes stiffen
Each stab forward a shifting of light

From shoulders, knees, as they wedge along.
A shuffling canal.
A black weight.
A star.

SHERPA TENT

The tent flap lifts
To a flash of tsampa-licking fingers
Caps tilted against foreheads' intense oak:
Faces so grained as to seem porous,
A cave to edge fingers along;
Stalactite teeth
Out of which laughter will burst
All jagged like an inundating sun.

WHIRLS OF A RAPID

Paths clothed with pines,
Walls no higher than knees.
Gingerly, a stream sparkling between boots:
With no need to hurry
I watch a whirling rapid.
Collapsing feathers, circles,
Compose the thin
Scattered om, hum, of a morning
Spent on some valley rocks.
May their jewels
Blaze in your name evermore.

The pattern sweeps by
Annulling, unencircled
Self in the onswirling roar.
I can see, not be; not both
At once. This is no garden
But rushing Himalayas
In their most acute
Irregular I you they us
Opening a challenge
Perpetually maintained in such a blast.

LAST EVENING

The tea house's coppery faces
Cupped by the wall bench might be gongs.
Trays before them, mostly bare.
A black fire-stained peace.
The chang bowl is drunk, rinsed
And perhaps another samples its wide heron-
Inscribed mist. No one talks.
Sweeping hands, wind-red faces,
A boy blowing flute-like into a grate
Where tea and potatoes steam.

I step out to a blackness
So transparent the quarter moon
Illumines the line of my path
Mounting past farms and bare fields.
Everything seems to be waiting.
I feel very thin, alone, joyful.

FALLING ASLEEP

I

The rowboat is my bassinet's pale blue
And stands alone in a fir-surrounded lake.
I notice a slanting path of sunlight.
Where it crosses the oarlocks a network,
Lyre-like, rises to intersect it.
Through shafts, two hundred yards along the shore,
Rungs of an abandoned diving platform.
Buoyed, I feel contained in forest light,
Only night's exuberant cadences
Awaiting: quick leaves, wind shoulders dancing.

II

Flying spume, curling bombardment, ever
Reiterated the same tall comber
Astonishing falls. A Pacific beach
I guess from the long run-in of the dis-
Membered beauty, the surge of froth and lace.
But the vertical splash as the breaker
Guillotines recalls the Long Island bar
Where as a kid I braved them on a mat.
Is it because that sentence lies behind
I can glory in this one tall, legs-high-
In-the-air, gardenia-cream explosion
Script in the oncrashing pageant of she.

III

Become my eyes I live in their tidepools
Harbored by their quiet. But no sunlight
Of a painterly sort has ever sparkled
In my veins. What can I make for her—sounds?

I pluck two old favorites, *stocking, shoe*.
A boot results, calf-high, green rippling suede.
The green demands, yes, a lilac meadow!
And the boot changes into that meadow's
Even better squat black juniper tree.

From meadow I mount until bluff shoulders
Outline a giant frog, hunched, about to jump.
But onto what? The temptation to peer
Is overwhelming. Succumbing, I note
A cliff ledge's bonsai-tiny cypress.
How far! I think, how perfect! how soft!

BONNARD

Notice how in the perception of vermillion
A crowd is erased

A PHARAONIC GLASS CASE

Blue vessels melt a peering tongue's
Pure wool

I see the pharaoh's death ship
Leave the harbor

The day
Is winter glass

High in a cage of leaves
The sun

Blue gardens are his eyes
A worm splitting into infinity

His fingers, drinking a dew
All blue tomb and smiles

WINDOW

electric night
breathes he who kneels
before a city unearthly
of moonbeam design
blue of hearts
and red of wine playing
with enamel earrings in cathedral
sun

BY A DISUSED
RAILROAD TRACK

ties you are what christ bore
the sweat dripping as he struggled
to pull it up calvary hill
everyone giggled at this man
carrying a cross on his back
tacking himself up hanging there
a fun religion
must get one for my fields

the children only saw horses ropes ladders
they stayed out and clapped
as the men tugged up that stone insanity
thinly singing between lichened hands

CROW FROM A
FOGGED RAMPART

idiocy's void beckons
how among such feathers
suspend myself

in the middle of
the bottle of moonlight
stands the crow

PASTORAL

Freeing solemnities:
Winter, night, day.

The chimney, aboil, stokes its pot.
Thermometers write away for sun.
I hold my wounds in my fingers
And they are taken away, swollen.
But doesn't frost bring a melting:
Bursts of paper, iron flies
Of sunlight welling from my head.

The farmer has a wheelbarrow by the hand
Trundles it through the barn door.
Beyond his pegged coat, a horse
Attached to its post like a door spring.
The silences move so they glisten
A wish rising from a well,
An arrow of midnight, alone.

The metaphor of flying is acute.
And lying?
At that red RED vibrations
Beat where as on an egg
A man sits, sunshaven, typing.
In a poem flying
Might be an Icarus released.
Here it tacks me to a May's

Single elongating frame.
Outside the country is blue
By hillside greens and red-roofed valley stone.
Sign to walk out
Drink the gold door of a day.

To a dream of shoes in wind feet stir
Where stone bench mutes an unruly prospect.
The ground is stuffed with struggling density,
"I'm the tallest," "no, you are,"
Argument in flower and grass and nettle.
Below, apple trees blossom, a few so white!
Grasses float to knee, waist.
An unfinished house thousands of stones old
Tempering my mist with quiets growing
Snails among blue bottles of periwinkle vine.

Sitting, I feel I can turn any day
To that bird whistle,
Mouth and hope and home. I want my hands
To know the long shattering of leaves
As burgundian blue turns to red,
Copper envelope, mist sun;
To squat by a shadowed rock
While the distance wells with names,
Wind's wonderful scissors
Cutting pines.

Risen through the orchard
A moon husk to light my way.
I liberate myself from silences.
As I step I am.

MAT-RIDING

Entering I stand, green as that beginning
When wave first flowered into child and I
Ran, my home those white umbrellas away
Out there among the tumbling casks. Those waves
May not be the night, but they come crying
With night's full fire and it's their lit skins
I have to ride, hurtling onto foam, sand.
When they roll me, it's whole eons ago:
Fish swim in my eyes, pebbles scrape me red,
Head bounces off the bottom, stunned, gang-planked.
When I surface there may be another
Bearing down and I must gather my breath,
Make sure I dive flatter than a shadow
Until the whole train's length has thundered by.
In the wrack insanity glitters, "Crawled
Out of you, wave, I'm crawling my way back."
Concentration is on this voice squiring
Me out through the slits in the breaking wall.
I'm coming home, home where I once belonged.
Ahead a path opens, I must, I will!
And chin down I hop on, flailing my way
Out of that vast dissolute cathedral.
Black-crack-moonlight-fleece and I'm out, floating
In the frothmill, feeling the wind behind
The shadow behind the blade. Everything
Is teeth, savage, distant, saturnian.
Mine are chattering, but as I hang on
I know what holds skier poised above a
Run, lover as he maneuvers his bulk
Till it locks onto that tumbling, shooting
Ecstasy when, like sheep, the waves scatter
And I shoot forth, alone into the night.
I want nothing more than to be the arc
In that fire spume and it is to this end

I wait until a breaker looms at length
Long armed and night maniacal enough
To ride, "If not for this, why have I been
Out here?" spur to set me paddling ahead
Of the racing engine. Then wave and I
Collide and it's *diamonds out* as the mat
Jerks forward and I take it, this wave house
Jelly-spattering me forth, barrelling
Me on a cushion of foam onto land
In a ride I never want to see end.

ICARUS

Reared in those bull-loud catacombs
I had no choice but to soar forth.
The island was too tight, its white
Alleys penetrated like stoves
Into my skin; door and you, girl,
Standing, reproachful shadow
Of my loneliness, knowing all
I touched would come back empty, an
Idiot cigarette, open
Jaw.
      So I left, melting up
On the soft candle of my need .
Like the skier fathoming through
The slow trees and absent birds, whites
That glistened like a liner's wake
Wax to the touch. Never more scared,
More alone. Even braving waist-
High hurricane surf was child's play
To this twisting myself upward
In a twine skein. Out upon glass
Kite floated, dew clangored in ears,
Bees came and licked my scalp, "Go home."

I rose, cool wind spilling about.
I was burning, but could not tell
So fast the string held me, so fast
I climbed like drum into night. High,
Earth became a disk, one vortex
Among many. Space grew wide.
I could not unsee, or avoid
Windblast hand crushing me to whose
Wine-dark intricacy I am.

ORFEO

The way down the rock stairs turns
And turns, all ellipses, curves,
Gliding intervals; notes piled
On notes, each step making one
More, one foot more in the trough.
How keep calm in those drear wastes
Bent on absorbing each grain
Even as voice throws it out
And the pigeons settle, only
To start up again, flashing
A gray day's sunset wings.
       All
Around a tumult of leaves,
Gathering phantoms, pressing
Themselves into the cortege
While down, key through shadowy
Kingdom, he goes in a gorge
Of pluming, spraying song. Heels
Are shrill windmills of splitting
Courage. Hands are knocks of wall
On wall. High, hollow rising
Voice throbs and there is only
The one echo, a going
Becoming cave, snow sinking
Into the soft furry fangs.

To have come so far and seen
Not even the dog. "Where can
She be—in bed? And where would
'Bed' be?" There is only dark,
Wild, frozen stars. And behind
The retinue following
Like a day that has no sound
Just a wingbeat to guide
Murmurous wasp center, alone.

LINES WRITTEN ASTRIDE
AN UPROOTED MAPLE

Roots and memory rises
a boy tumbling in grass
all of a boot tall.
If on the invisible side
of this straddled trunk
I could discover
snow! how tight
the leaves lace me, flutes,
flutterings—so tired
must run home now
·····················

The little print recedes
holes of a forest awning
I look up through
rumps crowns wingbars
so glad to be found
they're twittering like crazy.
Which pal taunted,
can't catch me, I'm free

Grin by groan rings spiral
until a forest stands
faces spines hands speech.
Open the book, make your hands warm.
Write on snow, I am.
Green
is marvelous destiny.

SEVEN, WITHOUT
BINOCULARS

Beaks, flashing plumages, feminine
cries, an illumined immensity
           shatters as I
crawl into the tick and bramble
infested next-door lot. Is this child
           oaf a new make
of bulldozer? A need to somehow
atone conjures me onto a log,
           a breathing stone,
unscribbled bark. When invisible
moss has grown over my face, and eyes
           are shivering
ice on a thin staring pole, I start
edging my way forward, a dime in
           a vase of wind.
My shadow sticks, my breath, a hushed mouth-
open, points at a silhouette size
           of a nugget
gleaming in a far crown. Without lenses
how wait for the telltale flash as she
           twitters and calls
but by becoming a bird myself
as I too plummet from leaf to song-
           lit life. I see,
no, I am the pond ripple where she,
grebe, dives and surfaces, stretches me
           to silk again.
Plunged enough in the silk I'm away
to the next bush of cardinal flame.
           Nowhere to go
but up! I exult, flat on my back
scanning treetop for warbler eyestripe.
           "In the next life

let me be you, flitting syllable,
only stay put until I've named you."
       Is that the gold
my wings glisten with, as if craning
a degree more, I'd no longer be
       this robin-named
boy, but a new ore bent on a bough
rod proclaiming a feathered lightning.

BIRDS IN A
FOREST SWAYING

Kingfisher

air appareled
blues the treetops
darting ink
in the blur
of survival

Redwing Blackbird
Orchestra Afire

reeds'
black
red
& yellow-
winged
brasses

sticks
in holiday
blaze
strike up
demented
embers

Blue-crowned Motmot

a tiny fern
on exaggeratedly
stretched wings
flies into the far leafage
dangles
wind & rain tossed

of everything liquid
the personal
blue
pronoun
sipping on uplifted
bough hot
sweet
green air

After Catullus

hummingbird swords
demonstrate as they scull
from one to the next heliconia
what sucking a whole flower
involves

Hummingbird Lech

A rufous-tailed
hummingbird

lights on an appropriate
heliconia

no yellow viper lurking?
before rowing himself

to his waterfall
singing perch

sky is his song's
absolute

it must be that blue
disconsolate

throb at the imminence
of an overtaking

note
night

whose homage
each must sing

one throat more sequined
quickening

then the last fiery
arrival

Riverside Wren

wren must display
itself or sing
if I'm to determine
its sex
that text
dwindling to conformity's
uncertain laws

but suicide
should not jump
to awful conclusions
the song
isn't certain to end
repeated
and deleted
wren way right
white eye-stripe
red
tail cocked

text
proclaiming
sing yourself

and the riverside band
plays ever more ebony blues
sending me up in smoke
hurrahing for you father
whose feather
warpipe taught me
to catch your woodnotes wild
before they detonate
dim late
to grass

Rain

canopy's penpoint
flutterings
presaging rain

appetites
ashiver
ink's surviving dots
dart
back & forth

soaking up
all the skull-
black sky they can
before they must leave

for a white
thinning abstraction

Nightingale Wren

love's frail rain-
afloat forest ark

survives, liquidly
sweet inklight

whistled nightingale
wren waltz, violet

revolving, bird
serene bride

MINIMAL DREAMS

Are blacks
Holding books between classes

Pages white
Elude them coz

Boot black with work
Page white with hope

Cross now where dancers
Select partners

Out of clauses between breasts
Lightning in yes, no, and nods

Forks over the gym's surging
Back and forth boot-crackling smiles

Arms out akimbo
Cocaine hummingbirds

In whose iridescent night
Unbuttoned stars

Eddy
Fragrant pauses

Of white
Discovery

ON PROJECT
TROUBADOUR'S
CAMEROON AIDS VAN

Slip slide to the equatorial heat
One two three four sardines to a seat
Smoked smelly yes! sardiney
Troubadours in dust-sealed glass
Bump sway shift to the shaking
Cameroon bus floor beat

Ooo! ouch! grit
Nsos those shiny gums
Grind driver those metallic teeth
Jelly bellies and tinkling bicycle bell boxes
Bounce to the jungle-jangle jolt
Of our unraveling can's Cameroon grind

Squish us abstract yeows
Squeeze ladies your voluminous circles
Kaleidoscope sarongs sun
And gun-loud shirts report
How cough point choke fire all zings by
Pistol shouts to Cameroon heaven

Ruptured outcrops purple blues reds
Pulsating pimento-flavored sky infernos
Crackle glittering together
Freedom unity 13 million unsquashable sardines
Rage in the age of AIDS
Pistol shouts to Cameroon heaven

DROPS

I

sandpipers   letters of air
in pebbles teetering
balancing names
      on colored legs
      as they probe
unmistakable mud
coots   kids   katydids
      fish the blue gum
washed   swimming
      swimming   washed
letters vanish
      mind of a water
      I navigate in

II

daughter's brush
radiates
moist extremes

not nets she insists
nests

geometries refract
the same flowing blue
      beach
where she stays forever
      shell
fish   tide   rising   lips
      pulse outwards
      breathe in
fragrances sea
      soaring air

SPOKE
SONG

velo pack's silvery
revolving
harmonic numbers

thin
ghostly ends
within hands' intense
slashed
lightning-stroke jer-
seys

zip over a wild
stone-
vowelled bridge on
the rhone

O

o my rooster's urge
to spring voice loud
inside that rusty lock

turn every chord
each lost
blue midnight key

to a vowel
dawn flushed
crimson screaming o

Notes

"Portrait of the Painter Kaldis" Aristomedmus Kaldis grew up in Lesbos before immigrating to New York, where he eventually became a semi-abstract painter. There is a Mount Olympos on Lesbos.

"Tapestry" Loukoum is the sugar-coated Turkish delight.

"Tsamiko" A highly acrobatic line dance from the Peloponnesus. The music for the dance features the clarino, a Greek clarinet.

"Zembeikiko" A one- or two-man dance in a heavy, hypnotic 9/4 meter. It originated with the Zebeik people of Anatolia for whom it was said to be a "combat with the eagle." The spirit of the dance is captured admirably in the film "Rembetiko."

"Wind" The coast is that of northern California, and the speaker is a woman.

"Looking for Binoculars" Ling is Nancy Ling Perry (1947–1974). A year later than the time referenced in this poem she organized the Symbionese Liberation Army, the interracial Berkeley-based guerrilla organization that murdered Marcus Foster, the admired Oakland school superintendent, and kidnapped Patricia Hearst.

"Intruder in the Abyss" *Dodalesquing*—Carol Doda was a topless stripper in San Francisco's North Beach.

"Tesi Lapcha Pass" An 18,800-foot pass near the Tibetan border.

"Last Evening" *Chang* is a fermented rice drink.

"Birds in a Forest Swaying" This suite of bird poems was written in Costa Rica.

"On Project Troubadour's Cameroon AIDS Van" The Nso is the dominant tribe of Northwest Province.

The James Dickey Contemporary Poetry Series
Edited by Richard Howard

Error and Angels
Maureen Bloomfield

Portrait in a Spoon
James Cummins

The Land of Milk and Honey
Sarah Getty

All Clear
Robert Hahn

Growing Back
Rika Lesser

Lilac Cigarette in a Wish Cathedral
Robin Magowan

Traveling in Notions: The Stories of Gordon Penn
Michael J. Rosen

United Artists
S. X. Rosenstock

The Threshold of the New
Henry Sloss

Green
Sidney Wade